KING OF BUSINESS

Mastery of Customer Relations Psychology

Abayomi Adeniyi Ajala

CONTINENTAL IMPROVEMENT AND ADVISORY SERVICES

CONTENTS

FOREWORD

In a highly competitive market, it is important to see the need to maintain a positive relationship with customers.The world has gone past the era of developing amazing products only, as consumers are not just interested in what you are selling, but on how you are sellingand to a large extent what happens after you have sold to them. This shift shows that consumers have higher expectations for consumer service.

The KING OF BUSINESS: A MASTERY OF THE PSYCHOLOGY OF CUSTOMER RELATIONS is an important book that talks about the challenge and solutions to creating an excellent customer experience that's consistent across every interaction. It brings to bare cutting edge practices that have benefited from deep and relevant research as well as the experience of the author across multiple spheres of society. It is carefully crafted to cover the full value chain of customer relations that are critical for driving the bottom line of any enterprise and the achievement of set objectives in a sustainable manner which guarantees a win-win situation for all stakeholders.

This thought piece takes the reader through an uncommonexperiential journey that begins with an examination of the key activities and initiatives that will be deployed by any business. Specifically, it x-rays;
- Who a customer is, the various types of customers and stra-

tegic ways to handle the different shades of customers.
· Understanding and meeting expectations, the seamless innovative and consistent ways to interact with customers
· The low hanging fruits in Customer satisfaction
· The Ws and H of Communicating with customers
· Complaint management as a principle and the elements to handling customer complaints.

The successful study and implementation of the above in any business will give one, mastery of his/her relationship to its customers, clientele and patrons which is the realisation of every business common goal. This book will inspire the creativity and customer relation skills of the reader, it will challenge fundamental practices but its implementation is truly rewarding. I, therefore, recommend this book for all those seeking to recharge their customer relation skill and drive their organization performance.

Rotimi Olawale
Executive Director
Youth Hub Africa

"It is not the employer who pays the wages. Employers only handle the money. It is the customer who pays the wages"......Henry Ford.

WHO IS A CUSTOMER?

A customer is a recipient of products or services which are intended for their use or required by them. Customer can be a person, group of person(s) or an organization. Terms such as clients, consumers, retailers and end users are among the various descriptions for customers.

Customers are very important in the production of goods and services without whom the cycle of production is incomplete. It is no gainsaying that understanding their importance and who they are in production and service delivery will give any business an edge over others.

Types of customers

There are different types of customers which are as follows

➢ **WINDOW SHOPPERS**

These set of customers have not made up their mind on whether to buy or not. They will engage any brand that is ready to capture and keep their attention.

➢ **POTENTIAL CUSTOMERS**

This is a type of customer who is prospect. He is not yet a customer but with the right approach can be won over. They need persuasion and monitoring before they become customers. This type of customers has already shown interest in the product or service but they need time before making a buying decision.

➢ NEW CUSTOMER

This type of customer has just purchased a product or service from your organization. They are still getting familiar with the product or service, learning how to use the product or benefit optimally from the service. Although a sale has been made, the new customer should not be left without help. A proper guidance on how to use the product and services is very important.

➢ IMPULSIVE CUSTOMER

This type of customer can make a buying decision in an instant if the condition compels them to do so. They do not need much persuasion before accepting to buy a product. Impulsive customer does not need to go through complicated steps before making a purchase. They need an easy and straight forward way to buy whatever they need.

➢ DISCOUNT DRIVEN CUSTOMER

They see value in any product and service they want to purchase but will not buy it at the full price. Selling the product at the full or higher price for this type of customer is not possible. Discount driven customer needs extra information on the product or the discount being offered. These set of customers want to be convinced on why they should purchase the product at the offered price. They will stay with you as much the price is still discounted. But once there is no discount. They will leave.

➢ BUYERS

The buyers are on a simple mission which is to buy. They know what they want and how to get. Their intention is usually informed by either recommendation or the need to shop regularly. Buying can be part of their job or domestic responsibility. Buyers, if properly handled can be transformed into loyal customers.

➤ LOYAL CUSTOMERS

These customers are the type that keep coming back for more after making a purchase or using your service. Your brand or product have become what they identify with and trust. Loyal customers recommend your services or products to friends and family. This will bring new set of customers your way.

➤ ADVOCATE OR REFERING CUSTOMERS

These are loyal customers who not only keep coming back to purchase your products or services. They spread word about it to others.

➤ RESEARCHERS

These set of customers need detailed information such as technical specification and detailed product description before they can commit to buy your product or service. They would have done extensive price comparison before coming to ask for your product. They need a lot of facts and details before they can be convinced to use your service or buy your product.

➤ DISSATISFIED CUSTOMERS

These customers are tired of advertising and marketing. They are interested in genuine information and good customer service. If your organization fail to deliver quality product, customers will leave. Not only that, they will express their frustration. With the advent of social media, any words of dissatisfaction will be said to and heard by others.

As it said that one dissatisfied customer will tell nine others.

➤ LAPSED CUSTOMERS

These are customers who have left your brand. But may not be truly gone if extra effort is made to get them back. This might be because you did not provide enough value, made them angry and lack customer service. As a result, they shut the door on your brand and left.

HOW TO DEAL WITH DIFFERENT TYPES OF CUSTOMERS?

There are several ways to deal with different types of customers. They are as follows;

➤ WINDOW SHOPPERS

Window shoppers need to be attracted before they can make up their mind to use your services or purchase your product. The more seamless or curious the experience is for a window shopper, the likelihood for them to be convinced to be a buyer. Attractive website, shop environment, proper product/service description and business premises can win over any window shopper.

➤ POTENTIAL CUSTOMERS

There is the need to let potential customers know upfront the value they can get from the product and services. This can be done personally or use the resources that will help them achieve them. Let them know that they can always ask for help or service advice in case if they are in doubt about any aspect of your product and services. They may not need this immediately, but they will appreciate the offer later.

➢ NEW CUSTOMERS

Explaining how to use a product will allow an organization to gain the trust of new customers. Doing this might require spending a lot of time with them or putting in place a proper customer experience process or program.

➢ IMPULSIVE CUSTOMERS

In order to deal successfully with impulsive customers, you need have a simplified process for accessing your product and services. This include but not limited to easy and quick process of making payment, quick response enquiries, simple and straight forward answers to questions as quick as possible. If your business is internet based or automated. The process of payment should be user friendly and simple.

➢ BUYERS

A simple process of payment will make buyers happy. All they what to do is to buy and subsequently become active customers. They do not need several advertisements blocking their path while trying to make a purchase online or a disorganized process of purchase and payment. The selling process should be as simple as possible.

➢ LOYAL CUSTOMERS

Loyal customers are the backbone of any brand. If any customers leave your brand, you can always count on them, come rain, come shine. Any serious brand need to make their loyal customers a reference point. Their experience should be a selling point for your organization. They should also be given opportunity to show case their experience to others. Loyal customers' experience should properly be studied in other to discover what makes them to stick to your brand.

Make sure their experience is always replicated with other customers. Ensure that whatever makes them loyal to you is not messed up.

➢ ADVOCATE OR REFERING CUSTOMERS

Advocates should be exposed to all the information about your product and usage of your service. This will help buttress their point in spreading the word about the product and services.

➢ DISSATISFIED CUSTOMERS

Your business should not be rigid. It should improve and evolve. It is important to monitor your customer service and social media channels for any signs of trouble.
Problems should be solved as they come, don't wait. It's cheaper and cost effective to apologize and offer small compensation than lose a customer.

➢ DISCOUNT DRIVEN CUSTOMERS

You need to provide added value that will make discount driven customers think twice before switching to another company. All the necessary details about the product or services should be provided in order to avoid any confusion. They may also require help with entering a discount code or using a coupon so make sure your team knows the product details. Also, offer added value to make sure they continue being one of your customers. You need to go beyond your initial offering. Add the icing on top of the cake. Something that is not available elsewhere. A good customer service can be one of such advantages that will help you keep them as a customer.

➢ LAPSED CUSTOMERS

You should not give up on lapsed customers. Keep all the options open. One key advantage you have over your competitors as regards lapsed customers is that they already know you. Everyone likes familiar things. We do not like changes. So if you manage to eliminate the problems, your lapsed customers may return.

➤ RESEARCHERS

In order to capture the attention of researchers and possible make them to buy from you, you need to present all the necessary information about your product and services. If your information is sufficient and convincing enough. They can end up patronizing your services. Care must be taken to distinguish researchers from competitors trying to gather more information about your products.

"If you do build a great experience, customer tells each other about that. Word of mouth is powerful".
-Jeff Bezos.

UNDERSTANDING AND MEETING EXPECTATION

C ustomer expectation refers to behavior(s) or action(s) exhibited or displayed by individual(s) or group of people while interacting with a company or organization. It is important for any organization offering products and services to customers to understand their needs and expectation. Customers of yester years have expectations such as a good price and quality service. But modern-day customers have complex and dynamic expectations. Modern day customers require prompt, proactive, tailor-made or individualized interactions. Understanding customer requirement is as important as meeting them. There should be a proper channel for receiving and documenting requirement of customers for the supply of products and services. In cases where customer requirements are not known or documented, it is essential for any serious organization to ask the customers for their specific requirement.

There is where documentation of orders and enquiries is important. The risk and opportunities that may affect the fulfillment of customer requirement should be addressed while striving to meet expectation. It is important to understand type of customer an organization is dealing before committing to supply products and services to the customer. Understanding customers' needs and exceeding their expectation is now an important tool for businesses nowadays to be on the competitive edge.

*Some of such expectations
are highlighted below;*

➤ SEAMLESS INTERACTION

Most customers want their interactions with any organization to be connected. The processes of buying or using your services should not be disjointed. Building on former interaction or engagement is vital to winning them over. It is important that whoever starts an engagement with a potential or new customer should be allowed to go on until the customer is won.

➤ PERSONALIZATION

Most customers needed to feel like humans while dealing with you. They prefer rather to be treated as humans instead of mere numbers. Understanding how to use the product and services you are introducing to them is important. Products and services information should be written in a simple and understandable way. It is also important for it to be communicated in the language they understand. Customers will respond well to offers that are tailor-made for them than to a general offer.

➤ INNOVATION

Any business that want to remain afloat in this age must be innovative. Customers will look forward to doing business with a company that introduces new products and services in line with their needs and current technology. New age customers want companies to offer new products and services more frequently than before.

➢ TRUST

Customers are more aware of their privacy than they do before. They prefer to do business with a company they are sure that their data or information provided will not be compromised. Customers prefer organizations or companies with a secured online payment channels to those with unsecured platforms.

➢ PROMPT AND BETTER SERVICES

Customers of this age expect immediate and responsive service. They do business with any organization that can respond to them in real time 24/7. In order to meet this expectation, a holistic view of customers need is important. Businesses need to understand the expectation of customers beforehand so that when they are interacting with them there will be enough understanding to elicit the right response. Any business that always match expectation with the right response and approach will increase the lifetime and loyalty of customers to their brand. Modern day customers will be more than willing to share personal information if they are convinced that it will lead to better services and enhance product recommendations, which is in line with their needs.

➢ CONSISTENCY

Several departments such as marketing, sales and customer service always rival them as to the ownership of the customer. Changes in the organization as to which department of individual will deal with customers must first consider delivering seamless experience to the customers. Customers expect to have seamless experience across various departments or channels of interacting with the organization. Majority of them tend to switch to competitors whenever this is lacking. The market standard nowadays is predictive and anticipatory services. Modern day customers expect organizations to use their data to provide anticipatory services. They want companies to anticipate their needs and offer predictive suggestions before contacting them. Customers of this age increasingly want products that are user friendly compared with customers of yester years. Companies can leverage on ability to collect and manage customers' data effectively in order to achieve this feat.

Exceeding customer expectation is not just important but also critical. The effect of just a single bad experience goes beyond just a lost sale. A lot of customers who had a bad experience with a company goes to a competitor especially when the latter provided them a better experience. Dissatisfied customers will definitely share their experience with their friends. The existence of online reviews and ratings of products and services is a medium where dissatisfied customers can air their views.

"There is a place in the world for any business that takes care of its customers after the sale". Harvey Mackay.

CUSTOMER SATISFACTION

I t is important for any business aiming to gain customers confidence to focus on enhancing customer satisfaction. What is customer satisfaction? This is the degree to which their requirement and expectation have been fulfilled. It is crucial for any business intending to warm it's into customers' heart to constantly monitor the degree to which their requirements have been fulfilled.

WHY CUSTOMERS SATISFACTION?

Customer satisfaction index is important for companies. It provides information on customers' loyalty, identification of issues with products and services and customers' decline. Companies that provide excellent customer service-leading to high customer satisfaction will always have an edge over their competitors. Most times, poor customer service and not price was the reason for customer decline. Excellent customer service is inversely proportional to customer decline. When the customer service is poor, customer decline will increase. But when customer service is excellent, customer decline will reduce.

HOW TO MONITOR CUSTOMER SATISFACTION?

Their perception can be monitored via feedback on products, surveys, meetings, report of dealers, warranty claims, market share analysis and compliments. Other areas of monitoring customer satisfaction are as follows;

> ➢ **CUSTOMER SERVICE COMMUNITIES**

It is not a bad idea to get feedback from a community on how an existing product is used or get ideas to develop new products. Advanced companies nowadays use communities' perception to develop or test new products.

> ➢ **TREAT CUSTOMERS THE WAY YOU WILL LIKE TO BE TREATED**

Customers are human beings with emotions. It is important to them to be fairly treated whenever they have contact or interact with your business. Employees should be constantly trained on how to handle both easy and difficult customers and business situation involving customers.

> ➢ **PROVISION OF NUMEROUS EFFECTIVE CUSTOMER SUPPORT CHANNELS**

With the advent of the social media, customers should be afforded various mean of reaching out to an organization such as web chats, internet, e-mail and so on. This will provide a means of reaching out to customers on their preferred channel. This does not only offer customers uninterrupted transition between channels but also prevent them from repeating information they have supplied to different customer support call center agents. Having to repeat information to different call center agents can be irritating to customers, thereby damaging the reputation of the company.

> ### EMPLOYEE SATISFACTION

The first step towards satisfying customers is employee satisfaction. When your staff are contented doing your job. They will extend same to your customers. Several incentives such as commendation for good performance, allowances, giving promotion as at when due and commission will boost their morale and performance at work. Training them on how to approach customers with courtesy and politeness is crucial.

> ### ALLOW COMPANY REPRESENTATIVE TO OWN AND MANAGE PROBLEMS

Company representatives should be trained to own problems emanating from them rather than escalating it without doing anything about it. It is only problems that are clearly not within their powers to solve that should be escalated. This give them confidence in their job. It also assures them that their opinion is value, they are taking their own action and positioned to deliver excellent customer service with minimal interference or supervision.

> ### ACT ON CUSTOMER SURVEY DATA

Whenever customer survey data has been collected, it is essential to act upon it. Good data empowers an organization to take action. The most important thing to do is to make sure that customer satisfaction survey is structured and conducted in such a way that it elicits honest responses from customers.

> ### KEEP MEASURING CUSTOMER SATISFACTION

A small percentage of unsatisfied customers will have a repeat business interaction with you. It is essential to always carry out periodic customer satisfaction survey. Doing this will reduce customer decline. It is recommended to carry-out independent customer survey with a service provider which is not part of your organization. This will aid getting honest and true position on your service delivery.

➢ MAKE PROBLEM SOLVING YOUR PRIORITY

Whatever it is you are producing or service you are offering? You need to know what your customers want and how to make it available to them. If all that your business is about is problem solving? Customers will be more than ready to pay and refer others. Also, whenever customers encounter issues along the line. You should be ready to go all out to solve the problem.

➢ FOCUS COMPANY CORE VALUES

Best businesses around the globe focus on company core values. They organize intensive training programs to sensitize and instill it into all employees. This is to ensure that all staff shares the same value and is consistently demonstrated when interacting with customers.

➢ BE CURRENT ON CUSTOMER REVIEWS

In this age of technology, customers are quick to go online to share their experience. This experience can either be positive or negative, the totality of which can either make or mar your business. Any serious business should take time to log on to the internet to see what people are saying about their businesses and respond to them appropriately. In responding you need to find out what people enjoy and areas where they want improvement. The reviews sometimes might be an eye opener to areas of improvement you have not considered before.

➢ PROACTIVE CUSTOMER SERVICE

Any organization that has the interest of customers at heart and is proactive should be the first to contact the customers before they do. This should be timely, personalized and relevant to the customers. Contacting the customers in this manner should be regular during the consumers' lifecycle. This can include reminders on payments, personalized reward & loyalty scheme and fraud monitoring. Adopting this approach will reduce calls from customers and improve the performance of company representatives.

➤ TAILOR-MADE SERVICES FOR THE CUSTOMER

Your business and services should be structured in such a way that it is personal to the customer. Each of them should be able to view your products or services as if it was made only for them. Streamline your business to suit the needs of each customer such that they will think they are the only one that matters to the business-which they are truly.
It is essential to refer to them by name, congratulate them on their birthday and wedding anniversary.

➤ REDUCE WAITING TIME

In today's fast paced world everyone is busy. Before any customer can schedule time to have contact with your business a lot of thinking and rescheduling of appointment must have happened. If your business cannot provide the highest level of service within the shortest possible time, they will look for others who can do it. The time customers need to wait before they are attended to should be properly managed and long wait be eliminated. Bureaucratic bottle-necks should be replaced with customer friendly processes. When customers discover that it is easy to do business with you, they will reward you with repeated patronage and refer their friends.

➤ HAVE A REAL TIME SOCIAL MEDIA PLAN

Modern customers need quick response to their demand in real time. It is important to have a team dedicated to monitoring the company's social media presence. This team should be empowered and able to give on time response to customers' requests and complaints almost immediately. Any business that is slow in responding to customers' request and complain on social media will in a matter of time ruin its reputation.

➢ **BECOME A CUSTOMER OF YOUR BEST COMPETITOR.** It is essential to understudy your competitor and find out what they are doing which makes them to have an edge over you. There is no sure way find out other than buying from them and becoming their customer. Whenever you do business with them, try and study their customer service and customer satisfaction process and improve on it in your business.

➢ **BE DYNAMIC AND READY TO BUILD RELATIONSHIP** It is essential for companies to understand the customer environment in which they operate. The environment in which they operate today is not likely to be the same tomorrow. It is only logical for companies to rethink their approach to doing business-by being dynamic as well as the customer and build an understanding relationship.

➢ **PRODUCT KNOWLEDGE**
Any company that will succeed in satisfying customers must have representatives with excellent product knowledge. Managers should take equip agents and reps with a better understanding of the product. This will go a long way in satisfying the customers because whoever that interact with has a wealth of knowledge about the product or service. A training plan should be developed to train agents on product and service knowledge. Knowledge of agents should be compared with each other in order to identify areas of improvement on one hand and identify the best agent to interact with customers on the other hand.

➢ **COMPARATIVE CUSTOMERS SATISFACTION**

It is not out of place for you to compare your organization's customer satisfaction with another company's own within your line of business or in the broader market. Every business has a competitor who are a bit successful than they do. You may compare their customers' satisfaction process with yours. Better still you can look for a company not within your industry who has an excellent customer service process and use their process as a benchmark. This benchmarking approach is an essential component of measuring and improving customer service and satisfaction.

➢ HAVE A CLEAR EXPECTATION

Companies should make customers aware of their standards and practices upfront before committing to doing business with them. They should be made aware of waiting time before they will receive response to their enquiries. Will the response be accurate or meet their requirement? Removing uncertainties about what to expect make customers to be assured that the company they are dealing has their interest at heart.

➢ HAVE A CUSTOMER HOTLINE

Some customers will not provide information except the have a means to protect their identities while doing so. They like to tell you what they think about your services and by anonymous while doing so. With this opportunity, customers will feel free to tell you what they feel about your services and ways to improve customer satisfaction.

➢ STUDYING COMPLAINTS AND COMPLIMENTS

Every message from customers should be seen as an avenue to improve customer satisfaction. Commendation point out what should be continued while complaints clearly reveal areas of improvement. Each message is unique in its own way. No message –especially complaints should be seen as just a mere complaint, but should be treated with utmost seriousness. No company should rest on it oars in the areas where they receive most commendation. But should strive to continually improve and surpass expectation.

> ### SCHEDULE DAILY PROBLEM-SOLVING MEETING CUSTOMER SERVICE TEAM

It is a good idea to hold daily meetings with your customers' service team. Problems waiting for solutions come in waves daily depending on the size of your organization. Having to wait for a week or a month before problems are solved might make attending to pressing customers' issue cumbersome. Solving problems should not be left solely in the hands of agents alone. Top management should hold daily meetings with the customers' service team. This will enable everyone to be on the same page and have hands on solutions to problems.

> ### ASK YOUR CUSTOMERS FOR PREFFERED CHANNEL OF RESPONSE

A sure way to enhance customer satisfaction is communicating with them through their preferred method. Some may prefer phone call, SMS or chats. The best way to reach online customers is through email. This allows online customers to maintain their anonymous status. Whenever customers receive a phone call from you, they may be surprised despite the fact that they supplied the information to you. Since this appears to be a more personal action. It is essential to have a list of questions to ask beforehand in order to maximize the time. By choosing the preferred method to contact them will give you a better chance of reaching them within a reasonable time frame, communicating effectively and achieving your target.

> ### GIVE CUSTOMERS ADDITIONAL BENEFITS

Customers will stick with your brand if they have unsolicited additional benefits. You can choose to surprise them with unexpected discounts on a product they have been longing to purchase or free after sales service. Surprising customers with freebies unexpectedly can go a long way in creating long term relationships and cementing existing one. As little as the added benefits can be, you will be amazed at how positive it will be for your business. It will also make your customers satisfaction index to rise.

➢ **FREE PRODUCT SUPPORT**

It is good to offer free training to your customers on how to use your products or services. You will not want to have confused customers who do not know how to use your product. Offering free training and support in this regard will alleviate whatever confusion they may have in using your products and services. New users of your products often tend to doubt their ability in using your product which they have spent money on. The support that offering free training on product gives tend to relieve them of self-doubt and make them to be loyal to your brand.

➢ **TREAT EACH CUSTOMERS INTERACTION AS SEPARATE**

It is important to know that each customer experience is different from each other. You do not need to use the experience you have with one customer to respond to another customer. When you have a frustrating experience with a customer, take a step backward and have a rethink before you deal with another one. You and your team should develop the ability of starting on a fresh page with each customer without any assuming that the experience will be as frustrating as the one you once had. Instead of reacting based on the last frustrating experience, endeavor to visualize the new opportunity that the new interaction presents.

➢ **CONDUCT FOCUS GROUP**

Invite customers for an open-ended chat and discussions. It

can be a meet and greet session which is devoid of any form of formalities. Try and make the session as relaxed as possible. This will allow you to set the customers in the mood to pour out their mind. Try and listen for the most part while asking them questions about what they like or do not like. Do not try to defend or justify your company's actions. Be attentive, make notes and thank them profusely at the end.

➢ REQUEST FOR MORE FEEDBACKS

Sometimes, it might be difficult to achieve customer satisfaction. In order to improve customer satisfaction, you need to go the extra mile to ask more questions. Most times customer satisfaction survey questionnaire might put limitation on getting more feedbacks. There should be a space on the customers' feedback form where they can type out their thoughts instead of just providing answers to your structured questions. You can ask a question like "what could we have done differently to improve your experience?".

By asking a question like this, which indicates that you intend to improve their satisfaction, they will be more than willing to give honest and insightful response.

➢ EQUIP YOUR REPRESENTATIVES

Customer service or sales representative should be equipped to solve problems on their own instead of escalating it to their superiors. Customers prefer to relate with someone who will solve their problems in the first place instead of speaking with a supervisor who may take long to understand the situation before solving their problems. Empowering your agents to make their own decision make your customers and reps happy and also reducing both customers and agents' attrition.

You'll never have a product or price advantage again. They can be too easily duplicated. But a strong customer service culture cannot be copied".
Jerry Fritz.

COMMUNICATING WITH CUSTOMERS

C ommunication is central to human interaction. It can either make or mar a business. Communicating effectively with customers can lead to increased sales, referrals, repeat business and reduce customer attrition. It is very essential for companies to plan communication with customers and clients alike.

They need to determine the following;
> What to communicate,
> When to communicate,
> With whom to communicate,
> How to communicate and
> Who communicates?

When all the five "whys" are answered communication with customers will be seamless and organized. It is not good for two people to be communicating two different things about the company to the clients at the same time. The appropriate time to communicate with customers should be carefully chosen using the proper channel of communication.
It is important to determine what to communicate to the customers. The following areas should be given a pride of

place while doing so.

- ➢ Information on products and services,
- ➢ Feedbacks on products and services,
- ➢ Complaints,
- ➢ Specific information on orders and enquiries,
- ➢ Handling or controlling customer properties.

"the effectiveness of communication is not defined by the communication, but by the response." - Milton Erickson,

Other cardinal concepts for enhancing effective communication with customers are highlighted below.

➢ PATIENCE
A lot of patience is required in dealing with customers. An irate and disturbed customer may be on the phone venting their anger due to service failure. They may sometimes be confused about what the problem really was. A great deal of patience is required by the customer service representative to understand the problem, be able to respond appropriately and provide solution. You need to be patient to capture the details of the problem and proffer solution. Remember, it is better to provide excellent service than fast service.

➢ ACCURATE INFORMATION
Customer service representatives should be empowered and trained to communicate accurate information to clients. For example, turnaround times communicated to customers across departments must be the same for the same service. When accurate turnaround times are communicated to customers, this will be used to set their expectations. When there is disparity. It makes customers unhappy.

➢ PROACTIVE APPROACH
Sometimes when resolving a customer's issue. It can take a

long time. It is highly essential and forthright for you to intimate the customers with the progress you have made. Do not leave the customers with the option of having to call you for an update. Having FAQs (frequently asked questions) on your website as the only option on your website instead of putting up a contact number through which customers can make enquiries is not a good practice.

➢ ATTENTIVENESS

It is essential to pay attention while attending to customers. Especially if the communication has to do with complain. Try as much as possible to be focused and avoid distractions as much as possible. You need to have a pen and paper handy and make notes. This will help you to avoid telling an already customer to repeat what he/she has said earlier.

➢ AVOID INTERRUPTION

In order to communicate effectively with customers, interruptions needed to be avoided as much as possible. Whenever a customer is complaining or letting you know what led to their disappointment, be careful enough not to interrupt. You may be familiar with the situation at end. But be patient enough for them to have their say. At this time, the temptation to offer quick solution arises. You must suppress it. Interrupt the customers make them think that they are less valued. Avoid interruption if you do not want to lose them.

➢ PRODUCT KNOWLEDGE

Customer enquiries can be about anything. But the most common is about products/services. All your employees should have a working knowledge of the product before communicating with the customers. There is no excuse for an employee not to be aware of the services their organization is offerings or the product the establishment is selling. The top management should ensure that all staff is trained and aware of the activities of the company.

> ## ➢ MINIMIZE HOLD TIMES

Most customers-including myself do not like to call customer care lines that hold you for a long time before a customer care representative attends to them. Even if the phone line is toll free-most times, customers get irritated when they have to be held for a long time before they are reached. You need to take steps to ensure that all calls are being directed to a live agent without having to be on hold for long. Having a properly set up automated answering machine will help reduce wait time. Also, another way to minimize waiting time is to set up your phone in such a way that it gives sound when a customer is on hold for a specific time. It will be of benefit to the company and the customers if they are told how long they will have to wait before a customer service agent will contact them.

> ## ➢ CONCLUDE CONVERSATIONS PROPERLY

Conclusions are as important as the first impression. Customer care agents sometimes are in a hurry to attend to the next customer. This practice can ruin the experience of the customer you are interact with at the moment. The eagerness to attend to more than one customer may cause you to lose more than one customer as well. So make sure that your agents are trained to conclude conversations well. Even if it means going the extra mile of staying on the phone a few minutes longer. Your main goal is to make the customer happy.

You may end the conversation in the following way;

1. Is there anything else you will like me to help you with?
2. Would you mind if I send you email containing the transcript of this chat?
3. Please don't hesitate to contact us if you need any

help in the future.
4. Thank you for your time today.

It is bad practice for you to allow the customers to sense that you are in a hurry. Words like,
1. I need to quickly attend to other customers,
2. Can you make your request brief?
3. Can you go straight to the point should not be used at all.

> **HONESTY**

Honesty works in communicating with customers. Customer service officers should be trained to work with this as a guiding principle. Whenever they are not aware of any details the business has to offer customers. Customers should be rightly informed that they will revert with the exact information. Do not give out information you are unsure about. Doing this will create doubts about the organization and the brands. If resolving an issue is going to take long than the expected, the customer should be made aware of this transparently. When this is not done transparently, it angers the customer. When the process that you will follow to resolve an issue is communicated with customers, it boosts their confidence in your brand and make them less angry.

> **CLARITY**

Communication with clients and customers alike should be clear, concise and straight to the point. Customer's time is very valuable. Your interaction with them should not be seen as a time-wasting exercise. Be it written or verbal communication. The communication should be relevant and address the main point. Emails and chats for example should be kept at a length that provides the relevant and right information.

> **AUDIBILITY**

The audio quality of conversation with customers during phone calls should be as clear as possible. Agents should be able to raise the voice to a level that the customers will not be struggling to hear them. In order to maintain personal connection with the customers, customer care representative should use their natural conversational tone during conversation with the customers.

➢ LISTEN ACTIVELY

It is important to listen actively when communicating with customers. They should not feel uncared for while the conversation is ongoing. Do not make them to repeat themselves. Endeavor to acknowledge the messages of your customers with positive comments. Let them have the confidence that you are there solely to assist them in the best possible way.

➢ USE POSITIVE LANGUAGE

Agents should be trained to use positive and empathic words while communicating with customers. Positive phrases such as "I will", "I can", "it is possible" and "I understand" should be constantly used by customer service officers. These words are powerful, proactive, encouraging, and restores customer's confidence and empathic. Customer service team members who use positive language are more likely to appease and satisfy customers than the ones who do not.

➢ AVOID THE USE OF NEGATIVE WORDS OR PHRASES

There is no room for negative words in dealing with customers. Doubt or uncertainty created by using negative words should be avoided like a plague. Words like "can't" or "don't" should be avoided in communicating with customers. Negative words or phrases not only frustrate customers. It also makes them to lose confidence in a brand.

➢ USE ANALOGIES WHERE NECESSARY

If you sense that your customer is having difficulty in understanding the solution that you are proposing. Ensure that you use analogy to further express what you saying. You need to refrain from the use of non-technical terms and you use simple or better still a language they can understand to convey your message.

➢ DO NOT TAKE SHORTCUTS

Be careful not attend let tiredness get in the way of excellent customer service. The customer you are attending to at the end of a long day may the your hundredth. But you may be his first customer service agent for the day. Do not be tempted to attend to your customer in a hurry.

"If you can't tolerate critics, don't do anything new or interesting". Jeff Bezos.

COMPLAINT MANAGEMENT

W HAT IS COMPLAINT?
This is the expression of dissatisfaction made to a company regarding its products and services. It is also involving the complaint handling process if a direct or indirect response is expected. Complain is not limited to offering services and selling products alone. It can also involve other processes where the organization interacts with customers.

WHAT IS COMPLAINT MANAGEMENT?

Complaint management is totality of all tools, processes, behaviors and methods used to collect, analyze, classify customer dissatisfaction with the sole aim of ameliorating and resolving the issue that lead to the complaint. The close usage and integration of tools and behavior indicate that complaint management is a vital part of the customer satisfaction and the overall quality management system (QMS).

Managing complaint is not just about making customers happy. But is an indication that there is a larger problem that the organization needed to address in order to mitigate risks, enhance product development and finding opportunities for improvement by meeting specific requirements of the customers.

PRINCIPLES OF COMPLAINT MANAGEMENT

The following are the principles that guide complain management process in order to allow for effective complain handling process. They are highlighted below;

➢ Deep and active commitment by the organization to define and implement the complaint handling process.

➢ Resources should be provided and it should be managed effectively.

➢ The process should be communicated to customers, personnel and other interested stakeholder.

➢ Customers should be provided with sufficient information about the complaint handling process.

➢ The process should be easily accessible to all complainant. This should include details of making and resolving complaints. The information should be easy to understand and use.

➢ The organization should be responsive in dealing customer complaint handling process.

➢ Every complaint should be addressed in an objective, equitable and unbiased manner.

➢ Every stage of the complaint handling process should be free of charge. No cost should be borne by the customers.

➢ The information about the entirety of the process should be accurate and not misleading.

➢ Customers personal data should be protected from disclosure except with the consent of the customers or is required by law.

➢ Customer –focused approach should be adopted and the process should be open to feedback.

➢ The organization should be accountable for and re-

porting its decision and action.
>   Complain should be handled and dispensed with as prompt as possible depending on the nature of the complaint and the process adopted.
> Competent personnel should handle the process.
> Increasing the effectiveness and efficiency of the complaint handling process should be a top priority of the organization.

OPERATIONS OF THE COMPLAINT HANDLING PROCESS

It is important to understand the important element in the operation of the complaint handling process. This is critical to the success of the process and the overall customer satisfaction.

> **COMMUNICATION**

Information concerning the process should be made readily available to the customers. They could be in the form of pamphlets, brochures or electronic formats. In whatever form they are. Customers, complainant and other interested stakeholders should not find it hard to lay hands on them.

The information guide should itemize the following;
1. Where complain can be lodged,
2. How complain can be made?
3. Information to be supplied by the complainant,
4. The process of handling the complaint,
5. Turnaround time associated with every stage of the complaint,
6. Internal and external options for remedy.
7. How the complainant can get feedback on the status of the complaint.

The complainant should be treated with courtesy through

the complaint handling process.

> ## RECEIPT OF COMPLAINT

When complaint is received, it should be recorded with a unique identification code. The type of remedy the complainant is seeking should be specified. Other information which should be included are as follows;

1. Details of the complaint and the supporting evidence,
2. Remedy sought,
3. Turnaround time for response and
4. Immediate action taken.

> ## COMPLAINT TRACKING

Tracking of complaint should start from the time it was received throughout the process until a remedy is found, final decision taken and the customer is satisfied. The complainant should be updated on the status of the complaint resolution at regular interval upon request before the agreed deadline for resolution.

> ## ACKNOWLEDGEMENT AND INITIAL ASSESSMENT OF COMPLAINT

When complain is received either by post, email, courier or phone. It should be acknowledged to the complainant immediately. The complaint should also be assessed immediately to give it a classification be it mild, severe or critical. The safety implication, complexity, need for immediate action and impact are very important in the initial assessment of the complaint. Any complaint about significant health and safety issues require immediate attention.

> ## COMPLAINT INVESTIGATION

The circumstances leading to and surrounding the complaint should be thoroughly investigated. The manner of investigation should be commensurate with the severity, impact and frequency of occurrence of the complaint.

➢ RESPONSE TO COMPLAINT

After a proper investigation of the complaint, the organization should provide a response either to correct or prevent future occurrence. If the complaint cannot be resolved immediately, it should be handled in a manner that will lead to effective resolution later on.

➢ COMMUNICATING THE DESCISION

Any action or decision taken towards the effective resolution of complaint should be communicated to the complainant or the organization personnel involved.

➢ CLOSING COMPLAINT

Whenever a decision is reached, the complainant should be communicated in order to find out if he accepts or rejects the proposed action. This information should be documented. In a situation where the proposed course of action is rejected by the complainant, this should be recorded as open, not concluded and other forms of recourse should be made available to the complainant. But when the proposed course of action is accepted, it should be documented as concluded.

BENEFITS OF COMPLAINT MANAGEMENT

Customer loyalty is a pivotal benefit of complain management. Having complaint resolved or eliminating it completely where practicable is important for an organization who wants to have customers who will stay with the brand and refer their friends.

" (Goodman,2006) revealed that unhappy customers who

complain to an organization about their products and services and have those complains resolved are; 30% more loyal to the brand than unhappy customers who did not complain and 50% more loyal than unhappy customers who complain but are not satisfied with the organization's response".

Whenever organizations manage complain effectively by modifying products to meet the specific needs of the customers and keep customers informed about how to avoid dissatisfactory products experience. They experience an increase in loyalty between 20% and 30% (Goodman, 2006).

Complain management is an important aspect of managing risk. Clauses 4.1 and 4.2 of ISO 9001:2015 in which risk management plays an important role included customers as an important stakeholder to consider in developing organization's risk profile.

Customer complaint is an important way of measuring customers' satisfaction. The more it comes the more satisfied the customers. While the less it comes indicates the more satisfied the customers are.

"The input it provides to the quality management system (QMS) can help organization to embrace opportunities for growth and innovation that are illuminated by effective risk management (Radziwill, 2018)."

Complaint management is a significant contributor to the overall customer experience. While many organizations continue to maintain transaction-based experience with customers, those that differentiated themselves in the market-place are embracing the Total Customer Experience (TCE). This involves the way customers incorporate products, services and post-transactional relationship into the very fabric of their practical and emotional lives (Freeman and Radziwill, JoQAT, 2018).

CHALLENGES OF COMPLAINT

MANAGEMENT

Complain can arise from any quarters at any time while dealing with customers. One of the main challenges of complaint management is the lack of an effective process for collecting and analyzing complain to facilitate resolution. With complains coming from different channels such as web chats, emails and social media. It is not unusual for organization to find it difficult to track all the information. These complain might be sitting and piling up in the email of a customer service representative. They may just be recorded in a simple excel spreadsheet. Organization needs to develop a process for rigorous analysis of customers' complaint, trends and resolution.

REFERENCES

1. ISO 10002:2018 (E) Quality Management-Customer Satisfaction-Guidelines for complaints handling in organizations.
2. 2018 Insight report on Customer Complaints Management: Drive Loyalty and Mitigate Risk Across Your Organization. www.intelex.com.
3. Goodman, John "Manage complaints to enhance customer loyalty". Quality Progress, February, 2006.
4. ISO 9001:2015 (E) Quality Management System-Requirements.
5. Freeman, Graham and Nicole Radziwill, "Voice of Customer (VoC): A review of the techniques to reveal and prioritize requirements for quality". "Journal of Quality Management Systems, Applied Engineering and Technology Management (JoQAT), Issue 2018, Volume 5, October. https://joqat.files.wordpress.com/2018/09/full-manuscript-17.pdf.
6. Radziwill, Nicole (2018) " Risk based thinking: Creating Opportunities' from strategic insights. https://www.intelex.com/resources/insight-report/risk-based-thinking-creating-opportunities-strategic-insights.
7. https://callminer.com/blog/15-surefire-ways-to-improve-customer-satisfaction/.
8. https://salesforce.com.
9. https://www.upliftingservice.com/learning.library/customer-service-contact/8-ways-to-improve-

customer-satisfaction.

10. https://netgate.net/articles/customer-satisfaction/4-great-ways-to-improve-customer-satisfaction.

ABOUT THE BOOK

Customer is the king so goes a wise saying. The rise and fall of any business depend solely on how customers are treated. The book is an attempt to make handy ingredients for the mastery of customer relations.

The book has fifty-four pages with five chapters. Chapter one was written on who customers are and how to deal with them. Meeting customer requirements and expectation was discussed in chapter two. Chapter three was dedicated to customer satisfaction and how to monitor it. Chapter four focused on communication. While chapter five discussed complaint management.

ABOUT THE AUTHOR

Abayomi Adeniyi Ajala

ABAYOMI ADENIYI AJALA is a technical writer, factory inspection team leader and lead auditor that specializes in quality factory inspection, quality management & food safety management system audits.

He has over seven years' experience both as a consumer complain committee member and Quality Management Systems Client Manager.

He is a PhD research fellow specializing in natural product Chemistry at Ladoke Akintola University of Technology (LAUTECH) Ogbomoso.

www.ingramcontent.com/pod-product-compliance
Lightning Source LLC
Chambersburg PA
CBHW071113220526
45467CB00004B/1851